AF414978

Advance Praise for

detoxification of the body

"gyukics considers three word-filled globes floating over his head, he captures them, ties them to his worktable, and using the golden needle that Hugo Ball gave him, he pierces them one by one to release clouds of words. Once they have settled there, he strokes them, thanks them, and hands them to us. They taste good, cherry soup or goulash in the cosmic cold."

—Andrei Codrescu poet, novelist, and essayist, NPR commentator and winner of the Peabody Award, editor of *Exquisite Corpse*, McCurdy Distinguished Professor Emeritus at Louisiana State University.

"gabor g gyukics' conceptual poetry, which employs outstanding compression, effortlessly creates and explores connections between incredibly distant and microscopically close subjects, is often compared to North American Indian, Far Eastern, and Hermetic poetry."

—Jiri Machanek, publisher of Protimluv Press, Czech Republic

The structure of gyukics' free verse is reminiscent of Ezra Pound's Vorticism, which ascribes a very special status to the poetic image. According to this view, the 'image' is essentially a singular moment when 'something external and objective is transformed into something internal and subjective.' These haiku-like image-moments cast ordinary objects, things, and events in a strange light, depriving them of their familiarity.

—Orsolya Rákai, literary scholar

"gyukics' poems are so beautifully poignant, as they take us through that certain "passageway of no gate," where the boundaries of space and time, the boundaries of you, me, us and others disappear, as if the memories of all the people who have ever lived and will ever come, the landscapes that have ever existed and imagined were all us /you, me, us, you, them / Every face is me; every face looks back at me and whoever looks at me recognizes themselves. This is the joy of encounter! The ability to communicate the unsayable without trying to force it into words!"

—E.M., a reader

"gyukics' poems reflect the way his mind is merging with English: he dives into the sea of language with greater courage, greater determination of an explorer; it's not just floating on a surface, it's squeezing sea sponges of their juices for whatever it's worth in any given circumstances.

—I.P., a reader

detoxification of
the body

by

gabor g. gyukics

detoxification of the body by gabor g. gyukics.
©gabor g. gyukics, 2024. All rights reserved.

ISBN: 979-8-8692-1429-4

Published by El Martillo Press
in the United States of America.
elmartillopress.com

Cover: "Geometric F(r)actures 200" by Octavio Quintanilla
octavioquintanilla.com

Set in Garamond.
Typeset for El Martillo Press by David A. Romero.
davidaromero.com

No part of this book may be reproduced without written permission from the publisher. All inquiries and permission requests should be addressed to the publisher.

NOTICE: SCHOOLS AND BUSINESSES
El Martillo Press offers copies of this book at quantity discount with bulk purchase for educational, business, or sales promotional use. For information, please email the publisher at elmartillopress@gmail.com.

TABLE OF CONTENTS

detoxification of
the body

recognition of ennui

the wind was lost in my hair

and fell into my shadow

on the other side of earth

in this invisible cold

questions lurk in my eyes

my organs slowly evaporating

their absence leaves a gap in the water

my face shows no killing intent

every wound heals on the trunks of unknown trees

the arches of the future disappear on their greenish branches

naked darkness multiplies my shoulders

my chest is a bed of miry leaves

frogs bathe in the pools of my footsteps

stories splash onto the shore's sand

every part of my body is a hired message

my features are a lost smile

in clayey slush

pine needles–raindrops fall from the sky

no one cries for the wound of another

I carry an avalanche on my fingertips.

earth grows wings on the sides of the mountains

and flies up to the stars that burden her body with life

the stones with our names

neither belong to

nor are magnetized by

any shadowy figures

the smoke of burning birch bark

colors my skin

makes my eyes water

tests the orifices of my skeleton

roots of clouds snake through my intestines

our innocence is based

on the forgotten dreams of the night

the roof of our silhouettes

overshadowed our decisions

the tree branches penetrated millions of parchments

our relationship might not be correlated to any behaviors

without heroes

a ripe pear finds its way through the branches

reaches the ground and explodes in my intrusive palms

I wash the goo off with fresh rainwater

collected in the well ring next to the draw well

the rain finds every gap

falling from zero point to zero

breaks through every heavy duty terrain

and calms down when it evolves

to become a stream that makes

the frogs quiet their croaking

the crickets their chirping

I place my palm on the ground

I feel the heartbeat of my mother

I hang the piking basket

to dry

on the hook of the counter brace

in the shed

not on her own

with lowered wings the wind appeared

she didn't blow anyone's hair

didn't flutter the leaves on the trees

she swayed beyond the fence

in the early sunset

camouflaged herself as a reflection

as if she couldn't decide

whether she wanted to be sensed or seen

she jumped over the fence a few times

looked around

and before an outside force

flew her away

she ran a fast round

leaving her scent behind

patch on the foghorn

under the wings of a dead angel

the moon is making love

to the sun

the negative of their bodies

lie in every riverbed

mountain range

dirt road

next to your footprint

in every ditch

by the walnut tree

you'll find a piece

of the moon

and not far from it

under the plum tree

shines a broken part

of the sun

visit

broken mirror shards cast shadows
to the boot sole dirt covered
ant-cleaved floor

mosquito and fly remains stuck
on the wall
faces hidden on the cabinet door
stare
at the abandoned room

through the window gap
the wind fluent in every language
blows secondhand air
at the musty walls

whispers something
to the body-wrinkled bed
waits for no answers
and lashes itself
to the cracks on the door

umbrella moon

you see your double on the water's surface
you lean closer
your body jostles itself inside the pores of your face
the angle is narrowed down by your glances

the wind won't dry your skin
in the deepening riverbed

you're thinking about a pleasant place
you've seen long ago
calming yourself
to get in harmony
with the environment

no need purchasing
a secondhand souvenir
from the thug hanging out
in front of the pawnshop
tonight

there are things
that can do you in—

a body

with a ripped-up abdomen

sinks faster

than the past with a mask on

cajoling present

in the swimming pool

he jumped headfirst

but before each length

he read a stanza from a poem

and during each fifty meters

he engraved each stanza in his brain

as many stanzas

as many lengths

when he finished

he recited the poem

to those present

at the pool's cafeteria

he left damp pages

from his notebook

in the locker room trashcan

deep sea calm at low tide

streams

creeks inject messages

into the veins of earth

rivers carry

the news

to the seas

and oceans

the gods

swinging their legs

on top of their belfries

waiting for the material to be processed

watching

deep sea calm at high tide

a hole in the sky was

carved by the moon over the ocean

for birds fallen to the water

the maker is searching for his face

on the surface

trees born again on the shore

the gods are laughing in their tongues

not a single bird

will get away

impossiblism

while running
the whirring of the sole of your feet
is the silent sound of a cave

the sky is angry
because it can't catch up with you
with your tricks practiced
for hundreds of millennia

only those can see you
who are about to die

you
down here
with straight up spine cajole
the unexplainable

and when the lightnings
are asleep
your silence is hiding
in the sound of thousands
of thunderings

nothing indicates

when it

appears again

surviving elevator music

along the polar vortex

a bird sings

she is the only one

her chaperone's hiding between notes

subfreezing road humps

turbulence in the vertical turned horizontal

who can make that out

washed up poets who actually never had made it

whose visceral quality is to be vilifying

anything

that is against their interest

ah

isn't that implicit condoning

a moniker

a mascot living in a brownstone

leaving all unexpurgated entities behind

navigating the terrain might be easy

navigating people is tricky

god

if it exists

has no need for our help

shindig

harvesting his memory
right after he was arrested
without hearing the Miranda warning
his case was accelerated
by two nocturnal detectives
ambling from sidewalk to sidewalk
luminescing nothing
except their boredom
and indifference towards the man
they picked out of the crowd
believing he committed a crime
they didn't know nothing about
yet
the man was different and thoughtful
which proved his guilt for them

ice dam removal

are there anymore stolen afternoons

on lovely boardwalks tête-à-tête

turning into bloody bay-walks

without warning signs of

stalkers on stilts rounding up slaughtered whales

and slaughtered pirates

everyday people are running the bridges

conning the Milarepa version on lacquered roads

subsiding the skyline and every cul-de-sac

with aggressive tendencies

while fake tv crews

decimating your beliefs in simple extremities

clairaudience

one can walk in

after the first frost

when ice flowers bloom in high windows

after the snakes hibernated,

when thunders went to sleep

an oblong figure maybe

whose curtains are open,

who has his blinds up

to see how

death robbed his lover's body of its value

pulled the last sentences out of her mouth

enveloped her dreams

to free them later

when they can survive like clouds

in pockets as fragments and patches

delivering her soul back to

where it came from

if her spirit would want it to go

meeting god after paradigm shift

what could we do
to make time slow down

sitting by the riverside
thinking
then

asking her to join in
to sojourn in every known space-time
together
the wind won't dry our bodies

ants are thirsty for our perspiration
every motion expands what we do

as we settle in the accelerated time

acoustic shadow

you are stepping on flowers

and gravel

among the railroad tracks

while your pursuers

are closely

gasping behind you

the arriving train

sets a barrier before them

their fidgeting feet

are visible behind

the clattering wheels

while you stare at

the train

from a water ditch

as it's leaving all of you

behind

small coffee with two cubes of sugar

furry parchments of the
unwound ambiance lingers
in your spider-cellophane eyes

the distance subduing
the sounds of mountains
is bombed out skeletons

the bends of rivers
the thorns of the buckeyes
the swirling of anthills
the droning of beehives
the silence of spiders
are dispersing gasoline stripes
of airplanes

and the sound of men
mocking god

this might be the moment
when
you finally decide

to move ahead ...

and

change your religion

spring

snowdrops bloom next to the anthill

the ants free themselves of their burden

dance around the garden

summer

wind shakes the trees in the garden
fallen apples thump the tin roof of the well
the maggots curl up inside them

autumn

quaking leaves
rain beaten fall from the tree
the wind rolls them
to heather-colored litter

winter

birds' footprints decorate the snow
under the pinewood branches
the crow accepts the pigeons

Bluebeard, see it?

Behold the imperfect city,

with your guilds

the illusion of organic waste

around the corner

blind pencil-salesclerk

her name is Freya

a moist shy host

her eyelashes are canned matchsticks

you'd take her in a whim

if you could

what is the origin of your being

you might think you're charming

full of spiritual strength

if you're wrong

you could slip on your city's

guild of bloody arias sang sidewalk

See?

all the faces are obvious

these are the invisible faces of the crucified

when you look at them

they bow their heads

earth's born from the battle of music

it's not an ordinary cavalcade

doors are locked

the key is in the hand of Yngvi

so your guild will fall

and the city perish

conjecture or else erased by suicide

silence slightly opens gives room for the sounds fussing
around

as soon as the sounds enter

they stop fussing

become one with

silence

the sounds stuck outside

knock together

waiting for silence

to open again

post-treatment

if you're a bit off

or in love perhaps

if you are angry with the wind

the rain

the lights

if an unknown burden weighs you down

dewy mornings give you no pleasure

the news makes you mad

then you think

that's that

it's over

you think

when the lights are shot off

then you can only visualize

your own expressionless face

because your tongue is smooth

every feather-footed noise makes you jump

that is when

your rapacious eyes reveal what you really are

yet the snow was sucked up by the same sun
that's growing fertile seeds
from the fissures of sandy soil

double identity

living in two centuries

not an easy task

you think

while still riding

very much in the

twentieth

hoping for a cure for all

we step over the border of time

I don't know

what you are waiting for

all I know is that

I'm waiting

for earth

to lose her

magnetic force

independence

you colorfully decorate

the times before history

chalk them up to guys

with fringes on their shoulders

you draw epaulettes

horses flying

to the caves of

robot dragons

you cozy up to anyone

stepping off a freight train

with a patch above their hearts

yet there are no news stories

you would share

with your local pitchman

present is god's sandwich wedged between
past and future

darkness and fog provide security

as opposed to the light of a street lamp

on the other side of the fence

stands a whitewashed house

unguarded

in the blade-mirror of god's dagger

a cul-de-sac makes itself visible

stalker

the tangled up branches
of this very heat wave
stab you with his splinters

if his mood allows
he diligently stalks your footsteps
watching you carefully

neither of you are set up
for deceit
the sun whispers a beam to his ears
the moon shines him in the eye

imagined birds
perch on nothing's branch

he's whistling to them
not losing sight of you
or anyone

token

cold as in a paper coat
at winter
waiting for the bus
but not getting get on
staying home

in your room
you know every position
of your shadow

in the afternoon
you decided to leave though

walking across the boulevard
found an ironed Franklin bill
on the crosswalk

silence remained
when the bus departed
leaving you in the smoke behind

after a downpour

the rainwater pouring down

from the rooftop

through the spout

gathers in pools on the gravel

flows over to weed-ridden sidewalks

the ground won't take it in

beyond nirvana

death takes the value of your body
along with all it had ever possessed
your name cannot be said out loud

the dead is taken from the house
through a hole cut on the side
of the setting sun

becomes immortal
when the living
talk about her deeds
when the wind
gently waves the Indian grass
in the reservation
under naked birch trees

resurrection from birds' point of view ...

every face is a white mask

shadows

are not glued to the ground

the spring

hermetically separates winter

from summer

shoulders are the wings of birds

and those who wish to fly

must sow their bones

deep in the ground

road to cold

the whip-cold limbs

of the river

snatch our legs

press us to the stones of bridges

before

leaving us to the vortex

whirling in different languages

after the storm

the water presently renouncing god

makes the broken pieces of the bridges

its own

in the red-less colored rays of

light

everything I can imagine is mine ...

clouds push the streets

down to face the ground

fences inflict wounds

on the clouds' bellies

behind its mask

sky's pouring down

most of its sorrow

every road is covered

it sounds

so

similar to the sound

of drums

its music can be

easily transcribed

simultaneous

the medicine woman
arrives together
with the moon

she heats up the sweatlodge
with her light

the herbs thrown
in the fire
will cure every
malady

Indian time misunderstood

when the Watersprinkler is playing his flute

on a 21st century tenement corner

where the sun heats up the brick

to the rhythmical sound of ripe pears

falling through the branches reach the ground

end up erupting inside your greedy fingers

bouncing on and off pretending

to be otherworldly plants

in front of an underwater gaudí backdrop

there, then and anywhere, anytime

consider and muse on the prospects of names

that might be nothing else

but references words when people are not present for
correlation not equaling causation in any

of the mitigated incongruities in the vanishing spring

while every other day

thousands of mantis deflorate billions of

buffalo grass, grama, sage, chamiza, snakeweed

so now it's time

to bade your copacetic moments of erectile sequences

and outrig the currently provided diaphanous life sentence

in every pond surrounded by fields lay in beds of red poppies
to tie the conglobated matter into something

that belongs only to your disguised self

among bunches of stinging nettles trying

to perform cunnilingus on an unevenly balanced

botanically active female meat-eater

who wants to turn you over

and gobble you after you finish

getting rid of your camouflage

wondering how will you end up

thinking of nothing in particular

looking at a wounded mirror whose host

never again will call anyone out on their names

to avoid falling out of its readymade

amalgamated framework of ground glass

greedy fingers consider and muse on

every reference word surrounded by fields
of stinging nettles hurting nothing in particular

*the fulfillment of a desire or else reported
missing by moving off the map*

the native elder

who lives behind

a wind-shaped cliff

on the rocky plain

erased the road

leading to his hogan

from the map

decorating a wall

in the local precinct

encyclical

this is the room

its scabrous floor
suggests it's more than just one

sneaking cold
surrounds them

outside

warm replaces the cold
tepid hailstorm swallows the light
washes the air clean

silence dies away
makes our voices
exchange
with routine tasks

tile shards' dust falls from the roof
blinding a staghorn sumac

undeveloped

we might belong to the light
listening to the sound of sky
in the revolving door of the night

where to find the border
in the labyrinth of the universe

in the opening door of the day
we might start
our mirroring path
again

our footprints
are visible
in the star dust

if he exists

his voice is
like himself
that's all that's known
if he exists

his saints' glories
forgotten left in the vortex
the lost memories of his apostles
somewhere can be found
he might be the one who hid them
if he exists

only hypocrites
and sinners
who have nothing to lose
feel to praise him
now and again
and commit thorn-grinned deeds
in his name

before it disappears
the inclining sunlight

gleams through

the slanted shadow

of the overripened hay

lost goon stick seen at the Amalfi Coast

the surface of the sea

is warped by the weight of cargo ships

around them the footsteps of Jesus

rain beaten seagulls follow his path

nibbling on trash and occasional small fish

confused by the splash caused by the soles

of his feet

gradually

the largest ship too

vanishes into oblivion

your last chance is a fishnet

hanging from the waist of Jesus

forgotten by the children of lost fishermen

marking time

in vain you step in the cage of dreams
your figure becomes amalgamated
in mirrors of specters

your physical bodies
stay invisible
no one can see them
day in
day out

in vain you shape your figures
to every existing occasion

all you achieve
is that you remain
inside the being
you have
never
wanted to be born into

frozen to polaroid

you plastered my eyes

I couldn't see
how you live
in different places
at the same time

I couldn't see
you watching
the zigzagging flashes
of the slices of light
becoming polaroid

among them
your only souvenir
the unknown gate of a garden
the only entrance
you could never exit

lying in the bottom
of the box
beneath your pictures

mirage

leaning away from the lectern
she watches
still she can't see
what is before her

her mother buried
the navel cord next to
the only tree in the courtyard
to keep her daughter at bay

on her weather and sun-beaten skin
the wind takes a break
in the empty
mile-wide space

in the raw air
blameless fog-clouds enshroud

her skyscraper solitude

in the cave deep silence
his may-fly long life

disperses in the mist

if she could

she would scatter sand to the

eyes of the thousand tongued wind

she stays alive

as long as she

laughs

in the midst of the

crowd

tranced to riot

the colors look different today

the apples
the cherry
the quince
are on the wane

the acacia
the medlar
the pink and the yellow rose
are blooming

swallowwort
and lilac grow among
withering tulips
through the windblown three branches
these flowers
cast a vivifying
shadowy image

crowed of ants hide in their undergrounds lairs
their red wrinkled slave driver armies

are not marching to gain power

just yet

under the branches of jasmine bushes

doves and redstarts fight off the cats

with the help of a couple of blue jays

the meadow grass is colored

with sinless wildflowers

as the forgotten castaway

enters the gate

permissive roof

music was coming from the attic

from the neighbor's reel to reel

when the ceiling dropped

and the flat got flooded by rainy water

making us stop smearing sweat to each other's skin

we gathered our slimy bodies to a corner

and watched the rest of the ceiling

pilling off one chunk after another

the cheap chandelier and the lamp globes filled up

with water from the sky hitting the roof

breaking through it

soaking the sheet rock and throw

pieces of it at us

sitting in foot high water

still watching the flood

processing further in the flat

again

we began caressing

touching kissing fingering each other

without thinking of the question

the storm that brought the rain

aimed at us

can't accuse a woodcock to be incogitant

when the weaver ants started moving

they did so

because something made them move

then a blue jay was affected by them and started flying

that effected a burrowing owl and

other animals got moving also

human animals too

were all doing their idiotic

and occasional

pleasant actions

for every cause has its effect

shift positions to ease the dying of bees

to ease the river running

the wind blowing

the trees answering to it

by dropping their seeds

to get into the spiral

of circles enduring

ink

today
the other heaven might open
where you could meet the alien

your ballpoint pen elevates to space
through the ink-red border clouds
while ant-like scouts patrol the area
the alien
is watching

the fangs of storm

not paying attention
while his skull tapped open
not looking inside
while letting the air out

that's that
it's erased

at such times
he might forget
to get on with it
anyway

falls nonchalantly
places barriers
in the cogwheel
leafs through the clouds
writes inside
onto them
with invisible ink
reads
until he is awakened

arrival

when cloud-haze billows
on raven wings
dampness of weather
cannot be fenced

the light
in the tale
fits easily in a casket
as the sun
the moon and all the stars

in vain
the native elder
guards it
in the depth of his tree-bark dwelling

raven finds it
steals it
hides it under his wings
flies to a land
where
he frees the stolen natural agent

where

every bird has a different name

where

every human wears an animal face

where

sound doesn't travel alone

where

darkness retreats

from a candle light

first step

you might go to the end

your name disappears
beyond the trees
drums playing

you're singing for rain

that hides in the shade
of the lines of your palm
as it begins to rain

singing the song
of burning sweat
in the vessels of the leaves

you turn translucent
the way a trickster
imitates manitou

guardian angels?

a pistol is held to your forehead
in a bosky alley of the night

you search for the face behind the hand
as you wait for the click of the trigger
and

instead you see
the hand holding the gun pull back

you take a deep breath
and when your lungs
fill up with the air of hope
a blow hits your temple

a stick-up
the thought enters you
together with the pain

two men stand above you
kick your face
your groin

repeatedly
without rushing

one of them leans above you

„you little piece of crap be happy
you're still alive"

perspiring at you

the evolution of armadillos

a speck of light runs into the speed of flashing darkness
unspooling the reel of time

anchoring the thoughts of secret languages

trapped in visionless eyes

making no sound

holding back reality's ability

not to lose its sense of creativity

turning shadows into utilizable

substances for robotic

nuances on unidentified

means of transportation

that can take anyone

to places were memory loss

is the key to survive

the often reemerging

actions of our former habitation

creating your own music

the early troglodytes might have despised

the shindings of birds

especially the cawing of crows

to beguile the tedium of watching the blunt-pointed angle

they choped wood after wood to pieces

chased thousands of mantises and cockroaches

from the greens of their caves

tried avoiding to hear the footfall of ghosts

by entering someone else's thoughts

parted the meadow covered with fiddlehead ferns

the surface of their long-built path across the hills

which was shaped by roots of every tree they had known
around the crevasse of earth

emitting particles of previously inhaled fog of density

when the thunders slept

they decorated long narrow sticks

with tales heard from wild horses

carved violins out of split wood

glued the pieces together with resin

used the intestines of a fallen once hungry wolf for strings
lifted all to their shoulder

and began to play

volumetric analysis

the perfect pronunciation may seem unnatural

in this ostensibly reprimanded formless morning cavalcade
turning into a shapeless day of an awkward evening

lost in a mute doorframe

leading to a private cloud of a colorful sky

full with goshawks calling each other

pointing out the plummeting temperature

in the surrounding cities where people

live off the grid due to introvert

blindsided authorities ostentatiously lurking around

protected by their frozen shells

without explicable reason that would make them

taintless before the spirits and invented gods of

the inhabitants

of

this

globe

rowing the temporal

as if a hundred years ago

and still

indigenous simplicity free from longing

we dive underwater by subway

from Pest to Buda

we rest

in the blinds of reeds on the shore

an osprey orbit overhead

speaking with his wings

a grass snake glides under our feet into the sedge

invisible frogs watch

dragonflies zip past

you don't yearn for anything

permutation of beauty sway in the breeze

no command

no pushing

no boasting

our eyes don't blink at material deficiency

in the footsteps of the past

enlightenment is such

a rare momentum

like the place

and date

on the back of

a photograph

in vain I stare

familiar faces though

still obscure

could it be the zoo

before

a donkey cart

by an artificial lake?

a boy

who might be me

standing

beside a fine woman

is she my grandmother?

not stopping short at two in one

a self-taught artist who made
a consciously forced close-up of your eyes
might think that

your arching unibrow
should be able to
persuade him as a gullible photographer

not to stop relieving his smarting incentives
as if they were accepted balancing acts
or overabundant majestic moments

that would ridicule adjacent blanket bans
manipulative vetoes and backfired missile attacks

after participating at the nuptials
of several lot lizards in midwestern truck stops
with cameras hanging from his neck

he wants nothing from you
only a picture taken to see every color
through the irises of your eyes

mystique movements

I'm standing on the edge of the tracks

the last train has gone

dogs bark behind closed fences

two girlfriends from the past

come unexpectedly to mind

their names are mysteries

but I see their faces

do they remember me

or do I no longer exist

I don't believe in time

Let it be past

future

present

I watch Spanish thrillers at night

these southern Europeans

can be just as

filthy perverted brutal creatures

as us

in our politics

or the Scandinavians

in their novels

the sky is white

the green of the trees is woodpecker pecking

I lie on my stomach

my face between two tufts of grass

holding my very last breath

the messenger

the bird-messenger

appearing for no reason

is unthinkable

as it was followed

by verdant patches on trees and bushes

what's this if not possible pieces of our madness

which appear as non-competitive details of life

emanating out of man

like most everything else

that creak inside us during winter time

and gives us serious strength to continue

that's why we're able to

chop iron with iron

piece after piece

helping us recognize

death as an acknowledgement of life

this is what throws us up without batting an eye

and fires our frozen engine

off to the celestial

burials in the sky

above the tree line

thwart unnecessary obligations

no need for compulsory rules

no need to outline the circumference

or to be harsh

or relentless

but to step on the path

on a rocky dais

follow a shallow ravine

or dry crevice

inviting scavenger birds

to the charnel ground

to feed on cut up humans

whose souls have

already flown

to the sky

light incongruity

calibrate your expectations

before walking through

revolving doors

to see ashes chocking

inflexible flames

erasing tainted rectangles

in the framed up fireplace

in a clearing

to figure why porcupines

have quills before

someone else does by

pretending indifference

as if they were reading

to the waves of the nearby

remorseless stream which

very recently swallowed

a nefarious grinder

with bloody remains

of a pedantic misogynist

who left his bindlestiff

in the virgin mind of

a female pauper

in her death shack

along with a

removable third eye

that has never ever

been shut

the ventriloquists

the inhabitants of this globe

will seriously mull over anything unworthy

that does not affect their daily routines

even if it let's them fall headfirst into a manhole

that won't ever regurgitate them

in vain they frown with relentless minds

or goggle at the particular absence of some staggering objects

which might pull them up

though there is no need

for ambitious plans

nor fractured sentences

on a mobile podium

by these disposable creatures

who are nothing but artful dodgers

for neither their ventricles

nor their hearing

nor vision

are omnipotent

hugging a robot

> you're the one who cut down the foliage around the
>
> > hanging garden
>
> yet it wasn't you who sent me the flowers
>
> but someone else
>
> who might be capable of love

all you need

is the scent of my skin

the openings of my body

you walk around me sniffing

like dogs around a bush

> you're covertly watching me
>
> hearkening in disguise
>
> mumbling your observations
>
> into your digital recording device
>
> listening to it sound by sound
>
> during your coffee break

later you bump into me by the revolving door

the dust stirred by our momentary touch

flies away

like an invisible entity

you wish to possess

> you touch me slightly in the elevator

which stopped a second ago

you caress me

like blind people read Braille

I crumple myself up

won't let you read me

under the ruins of the elevator

you're housing my whole body

profile

it's too early to start digging in the mud
perhaps I should wait to see and hear
which way the heart runs the blood
where on earth will be blobbing up fear

jostling the plummeting inanity crayoned
on the surface of cone anchors in the deep
among the paraphernalia of the ever-wicked
bottom of the oceans that could never sleep

predisposed, fractured sentences choked the flames
under the surface with light incongruity
their ashes almost erased all the virgin veins
of the streams running in mysterious unity

goggling at a particular absence of staggering objects
acting as artful dodgers with no need for ambitious plans
rewriting the nefarious nature of all previous projects
lead by a man who thinks he has it all in his hands

vanishing act

light dirtied his pedantically flinching face
the frozen shell of rehearsed authority
cannot grasp the significance of resistance
in spite of our laid-out world in a stretcher
his confidence is crumbling
in the gestures of this particular centrality

he is astonished in glancing at
 and discovering
a two-way traffic in his unadorned brain,
that made him lose his equilibrium
his benignity equals with fleecing
one can carry it anywhere
to conventional storefronts
to inconvenient staircases
to a convenient store upstairs
and leave it there as
compensation of an incredulous notion of
trap buttoned
confidence

hidden joy

an unstrained person

chopping wood after wood to pieces

in the swirling heat wave

shared by a shrinking sun dialing for the moon

to talk her into swapping

the day for night

wanting to set by gliding down a lake

next to the riparian marsh

among white warblers, ospreys

where the mantis is scarce grievously for the gliding leaf frogs
he who is incarcerated under a luminescent circle

closed to a sublime coastline

to cheer up the elusive wood chopper

he who is building a raft at the behest

of a swashbuckling superior

he hates

so he'll hide a leak he secretly bilged
for everyone's pleasure

concave manhole

shriek of a nail pulled from dry wood

is the sound of death's hoofs

covering a landscape measure

to reach

a wannabe constable

he who is hamming

behind a promisingly protective curtain of smoke

like an aardvark in the mud

we easily leave death alive

to get rid of creatures

unwished for

name your weapons

they cry

and those who rebel

will reach their demise

incomplete inventory

looking back

was it better

was it worse

you don't know

the quickening time

alters

rusting memory

in the spring of nothing

you can't find it

stopped searching for it

in time though

the crest of the highest stairway

might deteriorate

after the last one

he lowers the boom gate

steps between the tracks
stares at the landscape
above the contact area of the tracks
moves backwards
as if something were approaching
but it's only a flash of light

he raises the boom gate

hangs his hat
on the cranker
next to his epaulettes

contemporary human trash
covers the railroad gravels

he stands above them

no more train is coming

as of today

the railroad man with the yellow flag
and a long handled hammer in his hand
steadily walks around the empty space
the wagons left behind

along the railroad
reaching over the border
thousands of footprints
confiscated and thrown away
clothing and personal stuff
among them
a police helmet
stuck between the rails
trampled on

aim and look aside

the night watchman swears

the train never goes to places

where the river has no recollection

where the valley is the watch-pocket of the hill

where the pitapat sound turns to music

the train only goes to

where there are

possible offerings

where god

looks aside

a day on earth

The bloody carcass

of the dead dog

that missed the fox

was raided by an army of ants

they carried to storage

every morsel

in extended order

the poacher

didn't touch the carcass

he trampled on

the anthill

they're not afraid

a paper lampshade swayed

illuminating a well laid table

as the guests

shuffled around the stove's mouth

that let the soot fall back down in

from the brick chimney

the host

knocked out the dottle of his pipe on the strip floor

left through the window softly

letting his wings spread around the chimney

leaving the small crowd of people

dancing

drinking leftover liquor

the host watched them

with unwashed smiles

showing his barbed-wire teeth

to the smoke of his pipe

as the guests

are trying to figure out

their own departure

wendigos

evil moneygrubbers, shapeshifters, turncoats, quislings

backstabbers, usurpers easily make fools of us

for through their manipulations

we tend to believe every word they utter

they would kill their own fathers and mothers and children

commanding war machines run by racist hypocrites

and overachievers envious of our success

to point their guns at us and use them

to keep their stolen money and power

they rig every election

they replace and/or blackmail

the town criers, the mayors, journalists, police officers,

       functionaries,

all the judges with sycophants

behind whose backs they hide in fear their shameful gloating

now, it's time to drag them out into the open

for all to see

as they receive their just desserts

chaff

(to no one in particular)

I erased you from my past

you did the same

I won't let you enter my future

you do the same

after all

our mutual present

is no more

then a sec

sink me

the way you're strumming the guitar

you took from a pirate

with naked eye

making patterns to guide it

with irregular spirals

of languages with spontaneous

manners of the sound of snowfalls

and smoked roofs on fire

somewhere around one of

the incomplete oceans

with music heard from a

sunken warship and seen there

a convict dancing on the plank

not walking

that is when you realize

it is your life

hanging by a thread

makes you keep on playing

copulation at daylight

jaywalking is customary

in New York City

after all

red lights stand

in the way of progress

the subway is running

on its own time

only occasional floods

can alter the system

sun and rain come down

together smoothly

raindrops and sun-sweat

making love

on my forehead

totem

the skyscrapers on the streets

with Indian names

aren't occupied by first nation people

rather by window washers

and security contractors

they are the twelve-tone technique of the scale

occasionally

one can hear

the breathing of invisible Indians

and smell the scent of earth

scattered on the asphalt

from their moccasins

in the cities

too bright

I reflect the world

some part of it for certain

I see her coming

she'll never arrive

I see her leaving

she'll never depart

ABOUT THE AUTHOR

gabor g. gyukics (b. 1958) poet, jazz poet, literary translator born in Budapest, Hungary. He is the author of 11 books of original poetry, 6 in Hungarian, 2 in English, 1 in Arabic, 1 in Czech, 1 in Bulgarian and 19 translations including *A Transparent Lion*, selected poetry of Attila József (2006), Green Integer Press and *They'll Be Good for Seed: Anthology of Hungarian Poetry* (2021) (in English, both with co-translator Michael Castro) White Pine Press and an anthology of North American Indigenous poets in Hungarian titled *Medvefelhő a város felett* (2015) Scolar Publishing.

He writes his poems in English (which is his second language) and Hungarian. He lived in Holland for two years before moving to the US where he lived from 1988-2002. At present, he resides in Szeged, Hungary.

His poetic works and translations have been published in hundreds of magazines and anthologies in English, Hungarian, and other languages worldwide. He is a recipient of the Banff International Literary Translation Centre (BILTC) residency in Canada in 2011.

a hermit has no plural, a collection of poems in English, was published by Singing Bone Press in the fall of 2015. His latest book in Hungarian titled *végigtapint* was published by Lector Press in May 2018.

In September 2020, he received the Hungary Beat Poet Laureate Lifetime award by the National Beat Poetry Foundation Inc. USA.

ABOUT THE ARTIST

Octavio Quintanilla is the author of the poetry collection, *If I Go Missing* (Slough Press, 2014) and served as the 2018-2020 Poet Laureate of San Antonio, TX. His Frontextos (visual poems) have been published in *Poetry Northwest, Gold Wake Live, Newfound, Chachalaca Review, Chair Poetry Evenings, Red Wedge, The Museum of Americana, About Place Journal, The American Journal of Poetry, The Windward Review, Tapestry, Twisted Vine Literary Arts Journal,* & *The Langdon Review of the Arts* in Texas.

Octavio's visual work has been exhibited at the Southwest School of Art, Presa House Gallery, Equinox Gallery, UTRGV-Brownsville, the Weslaco Museum, Aanna Reyes Gallery in San Antonio, TX, Our Lady of the Lake University, AllState Almaguer art space in Mission, El Centro Cultural Hispano de San Marcos, The Walker's Gallery in San Marcos, TX, and in the Emma S. Barrientos Mexican American Cultural Center / Black Box Theater in Austin, TX. He holds a Ph.D. from the University of North Texas and is the regional editor for *Texas Books in Review* and poetry editor for *The Journal of Latina Critical Feminism* & for *Voices de la Luna: A Quarterly Literature & Arts Magazine.* Octavio teaches Literature and Creative Writing in the M.A./M.F.A. program at Our Lady of the Lake University in San Antonio, Texas.

ACKNOWLEDGMENTS

The poet thanks the following magazines and anthologies for previously publishing some of these poems included in this book:

Sensitive Skin, Whirlwind, In-Flight, Jazz Cigarette now Petrichor, Shantih, Subterranean Blue, Yellow Medicine Review, All the Sins, The Lake, Red Ink - International Journal of Indigenous Literature, Tsunami Books, Panel, Writer's Café, Taj Mahal Review, Ostrava Journal of English Philology, The Blue Nib, Bezine, San Francisco Public Library – Poem of the Day, Sutterville Review, Poetrybay.com, Red Fern Review, About Place Journal, Silkworm, The Opiate Magazine, Lothlorien Poetry Journal, The Fringe Poetry Magazine, Copihue Poetry Magazine, Alien Buddha Press, Edgar Allan Poet Journal, MadHat Lit, Silver Birch Press, Episteme, DoveTales, Fox Adoption Magazine, Atelier Poesi Press, WordCity Literary Journal, Madness Anthology, Earth: Dig It: New Generation Beat Poets Laureate Anthology, A Wreath of Golden Laurels: An Anthology of Poetry by 100 Poets Laureate, Remembering Jack Kerouac on His 100th Birthday Anthology, My Daisies from the Side of the Road - A Collective Tribute to Maurice Kenny, and *The Salerno Project 3.*

The poet would like to thank:

David A. Romero, Matt Sedillo, Anna Lombardo, Angela Galli, Susanne Johnston, Patrick Harford, Will Alexander, Kim Schuck, Andrei Codrescu, Orsolya Rákai, Éva Muhi, Irina Perish, Mark Lipman, and Octavio Quintanilla.

Founded by Matt Sedillo and David A. Romero, El Martillo Press publishes writers whose pens strike the page with clear intent; words with purpose to pry apart assumed norms and to hammer away at injustice. El Martillo Press proactively publishes writers looking to pound the pavement to promote their work and the work of their fellow pressmates. El Martillo is the builder of bridges and the destroyer of walls.

El Martillo Press titles:

- *detoxification of the body* by gabor g. gyukics
- *Blackout* by Anna Lombardo
- *From Venice to Venice: Poets of California and Italy*
  edited by Mark Lipman and Anna Lombardo
- *A Crown of Flames: Selected Poems & Aphorisms* by Flaminia Cruciani
- *Paper Birds: Feather by Feather / Pájaros de papel: pluma por pluma*
  by Sonia Gutiérrez
- *All Brown Boys Get Trumpets* by Matthew Cuban Hernandez
- *Chimeras Dream on Barren Lands* by Alex Alpharaoh
- *the daughterland* by Margaret Elysia Garcia
- *WE STILL BE: Poems and Performances* by Paul S. Flores
- *Touch the Sky by Donato Martinez*

To purchase these books and to keep up with new titles, visit elmartillopress.com.